Corinne Boyer Fund

presents

Ben Wicks

on

Ovarian Cancer

Published in 1998 by
Ben Wicks and Associates
449A Jarvis Street
Toronto, Ontario
M4Y 2G8

Important information about ovarian cancer
is contained in this book. It is a guide and
not a protection guarantee.

Foreword

Dear Reader,

Corinne Boyer, full of vitality and determination, kept ahead of cancer for 17 years, overcoming it with her determination, her knowledge, and especially her optimistic brightness to prevail -- like a sunflower.

Following Corinne's death in 1995, we created the Corinne Boyer Fund to advance ovarian cancer research and treatment. The sunflower is our symbol.

The money we raise is already funding medical research on new approaches for early detection. Our work is directed to prevention, earlier detection, more successful treatment, and continuous supportive care for women with this disease and their families. Education and awareness are a big part of our comprehensive campaign against cancer of the ovary.

If awareness is key, who better to get your attention than Ben Wicks? This masterful communicator's renowned humour takes us, on these following pages, into that delicate realm where what we fear is met by that defiant and endearing human quality he can trigger so well.

Humour is about the indomitable side of the human character. Corinne used to say we all look more beautiful when we smile. She also said, "Don't be passive!"

So smile, then act!

Patrick Boyer, Q.C.
Chair, Corinne Boyer Fund

Contents

INTRODUCTION · 5

1   So This Is Me · 13

2   What Are The Ovaries And
    Where Are They? · 23

3   Ovarian Cancer · 31

4   What Are The Signs To Watch
    For? · 39

5   Who Is At Risk? · 51

6   Friend Or Foe? · 58

7   Treatment · 67

8   Getting The Right Doctor · 73

9   You Still Have A Life To Lead · 83

10 What Happens Next? · 91

Introduction

Of all the diseases that are skulking around waiting to attack the first person that passes by, few strike more fear into the human being than the disease known as cancer.

Although incredible advances have been made in the treatment of this disease, for some cancers, there is a long road to travel before an actual cure can be found.

Those who sat and listened to a doctor give them the news that they feared the most will never forget that feeling of absolute helplessness.

What they have been told is devastating and, what is worse, they feel that there is little they can do personally to reverse the situation.

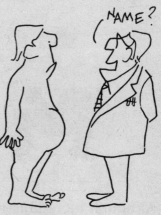

Their fate appears to lie in the hands of another: a person who all too often wears a white coat and is a complete stranger.

For many patients, the doctor will quickly reassure them with the news that things are not always as serious as they may have first thought.

In which case, working together will soon help correct any setbacks the body is experiencing at the time.

For others, the news can indeed be serious and they may require extensive treatment in order to get back into a healthy state.

Ovarian cancer is serious: serious enough to require more than a take-this-pill-three-times-a-day-and-come-back-to-see-me-next-week treatment.

Those who have survived ovarian cancer, and there are many, would quickly attest to this fact. The disease has resulted in the deaths of many women; however, those who have survived are also high in numbers.

My wife, who was diagnosed with ovarian cancer four years ago, has

once again received a clean
bill of health from her
latest examination.

Some weeks ago,
I was the guest
speaker at a
senior citizens
function. During
the evening, one of
the women who was
aware of Doreen's
illness asked how she was.

"Fortunately," I answered, "she is
fine and feels very fortunate in view
of the seriousness of her illness."

"I know just how she feels," the
women said. "I had ovarian cancer
thirty years ago and I feel just
great!"

The fact is that no two people with the

same form of cancer will necessarily experience an identical result.

The treatment for some can be as devastating as the first time they heard the news.

Others will find that their treatment has little effect on their bodies and that they are able to carry on doing whatever it was they did, with little discomfort.

Each person will cope with her illness in different ways. There will be times of deep anxiety for those with cancer and for their close friends and relatives. This is to be expected. Anyone diagnosed with ovarian cancer will be anxiously searching for information on this type of cancer.

They will feel the same sense of dread as that experienced by early man who refused to enter a cave for fear of what lay waiting in the dark.

It is my heartfelt wish that this book will light the cave in which the animal we call Ovarian Cancer lurks. In so doing, this book will give the reader the knowledge needed to help overcome the fears associated with the disease.

1 SO THIS IS ME

It's astonishing how ignorant we are
of our own bodies. We drag them
around with us day after day
and few of us bother to
appreciate what a
miraculous piece of
machinery it really is.

In fact, as with
most pieces of
machinery, few of us
bother to find out what
makes us tick until such time
as we experience a break down.

Before beginning to find out what cancer is and why it can damage the inner workings of our bodies so effectively, let's open a mouth, pop inside and have a look at the incredible inner workings of this thing called a body.

OPEN WIDE, WE'RE COMING IN!

Whether we're built like Mel Gibson or Joan Rivers, each of us began our existence in the same way -- with a single cell.

From this tiny beginning, millions of cells began sloshing their way around the body, each of them with a specific job to do.

The wonderful news is that when these little workers decide that it's time to put their feet up for a well-earned rest, other cells are ready to take their place.

Where do these new cells come from? That's simple. The original cells divide to produce new cells just raring to do their bit and carry on where the old cells left off.

Unfortunately, like workers everywhere, the replacements are not always up to the task of doing as good a job as the cells they replaced.

To make matters worse, this bunch of rebel cells begins to divide and produce another bunch of good-for-nothing lay-abouts.

These are cells that couldn't care less about the job they have been directed to do.

Before you can blink an eye, this crowd of renegade cells start walloping around the body, pushing and shoving those cells who just want to be left alone to do their good work.

USELESS CELLS

DECENT CELLS

With no one around to stop them, this gang of ruffians begins to grow to such an extent that the normal cells are completely squeezed out of the picture.

They are, in fact, like a foreign army and like all foreign armies they have a name. This army is called a tumour.

Before you start throwing stones at this tumour, you should know that there are two types of tumour armies.

One lot, the Benign army, generally stays within its own borders, with no real desire to colonize.

Frankly, this army can be easily dealt with.

Our problem is with the second army. This group, the Malignant ones, is a very different kettle of fish.

Not only are they an unruly mob, they all too often decide to move across their own borders to begin to invade other areas and cause all manner of problems.

CHARGE!

Like an evil dictator giving out orders to his supporters, this malignant tumour will soon be instructing the rotten cells to break away from the main force to cross the neighbouring borders into areas of the body where they have no right to settle.

Once they arrive, they set up camp and begin to multiply.

What was once a small scouting group has now become a force that needs to be dealt with -- a force that has multiplied.

It is so out of control that this gang is soon increasing its membership. In fact, it is growing to such a degree that most healthy tissues that dare to cross its path are quickly destroyed.

Having broken away from their 'home base', these pieces of tumour are now on a wild ride.

They need no flags or identifying markings. Their very actions signify who they are. They are what is commonly known as a malignant tumour.

TODAY
I FOUND OUT
WHERE THE
OVARIES ARE—
WOW!

2 WHAT ARE THE OVARIES AND WHERE ARE THEY?

Actually, there are two of them. Each is the size and shape of an almond nut.

To find them, you'll need to look on either side of the uterus, just below the ends of the fallopian tubes.

THEY'RE HERE!

Without these little beauties, the human race would be a figment of some higher being's imagination.

Every month these little critters called ovaries respond to a signal from the pituitary gland and release an egg ready for fertilization.

LET GO -ONE EGG

It's no surprise to find that a complicated act such as this will occasionally run into a problem.

One of the most common problems occurs when a cyst filled with fluid rises out of a small sack called a follicle and decides to misbehave.

The end result can be an ovarian
cyst that has grown to the
size of a lemon: not
the kind of thing
anyone wants
to carry
around
inside
her.

Although it's hard to believe, this
can occur without the body's
signalling that it is happening.

The first sign of a problem can be
when a cyst has grown to such a
size that a woman can begin to feel
a dull ache or pain in the pelvic area.

Happily, small cysts usually decide
that after hanging around for a short
period, it's time to disappear. They
often do so after a couple of
menstrual cycles.

Knowing this, a doctor will usually recommend that the patient return in a couple of months.

If, after an examination, the doctor finds that the cyst is still there and has grown, he or she will usually recommend surgery to get rid of the problem.

Yet another kind of cyst is called by a classy name, Dermoid cyst.

Believe it or not, this common, benign ovarian tumour contains either teeth, hair or sweat glands.

There since birth, these dermoid cysts are an example of a small error made when we were just an embryo.

The biggest problem with these little terrors is that the cyst can burst or twist, causing pain. Should this happen, you will require surgery to fix the problem.

The good news about these two characters is that they are rarely malignant.

They are quite happy to stay on their side of the border or until a  time when they retire or are plucked out by the surgeon's knife.

This is not to suggest that having a cyst removed is a comfortable experience.

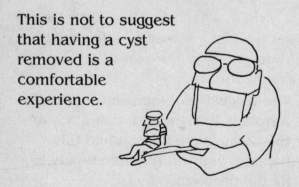

Some benign ovarian tumors can get incredibly large. There was one on record that weighed 22.5 pounds. This is not the kind of cyst to treat with a band-aid.

So much for the kind of tumours that are quite happy to hang around their own neighbourhood.

It's now time to gather information about a much more dangerous enemy force.

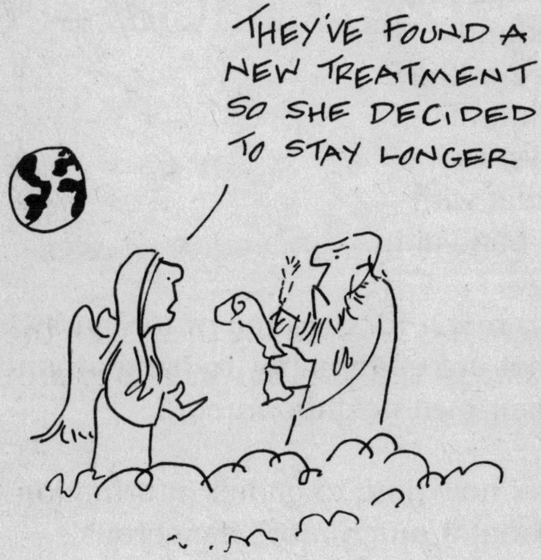
THEY'VE FOUND A NEW TREATMENT SO SHE DECIDED TO STAY LONGER

3 OVARIAN CANCER

There are more than 200 types of cancers. The simple way to identify them has been to tag them with the name of the area in which they are found.

Of this large number of various cancers, many are easily dealt with for the simple reason that they're not difficult to detect.

The first sign of their presence will be a change in the health of the person. In many cases, this can be a pain that signifies where the growth is located, or, as in the case of skin cancer, a small mole or discolouring of the skin.

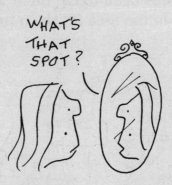

Once a cancerous growth has made its presence known, treating that growth can be started and, in many cases, treated successfully.

There are, however, areas of the body in which a cancer can successfully invade, with little chance of detection, until the invading army has settled in and is difficult to dislodge.

Such a hiding place is in the ovaries, located deep inside the body. Here, cancer can be hard to detect during a regular checkup.

It's true that a doctor can feel the ovaries during a pelvic examination but, in many cases, detection of a lump signals that the growth is already large enough to present a serious problem.

Since the location of the ovaries is fairly remote, it makes it a perfect jumping off place for the enemy that has settled in the area.

Malignant cells that break away from the tumour are soon heading off for other parts of the body.

Like invading armies everywhere,
the attraction usually lies with those
whose borders are
closest and,
therefore,
easiest to
reach.

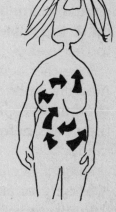

Certainly, the
other ovary
can become
a prime
target.

Other attractive
points for the ovarian
cancer break-away cells are
the fallopian tubes, the uterus and
any or all other organs that are
located in the abdominal cavity.

Unfortunately, left untreated, these
villainous cells will press onward.

The ovarian malignant cells soon have their eyes on other vital areas. In no time at all, they can head for the lining of the abdomen or lymph glands at the back of the abdomen, up to the lining of the lungs or even to the liver.

Actually, in over 70% of cases, this ovarian disease has spread beyond the pelvis before the diagnosis is made.

A close examination of the cells from these tumours will determine  whether or not the malignancy is an offshoot of ovarian cancer or began its journey from somewhere else.

The good news is that, although this vicious enemy has already crossed a boundary of our body, if dealt with early enough, there would still be time to strike back and deal with the problem.

GOOD
GUYS

4 WHAT ARE THE SIGNS TO WATCH FOR?

So much for all the talk about what ovarian cancer is.

Since ovarian cancer is so difficult to detect early, what might some of the red flags be?

You may feel that since you go regularly for a checkup, ovarian cancer would never fool your doctor. I'm sorry to disappoint you but, as brilliant as your doctor may be, the task is pretty daunting.

The difficulty is getting a close look at what the problem may be. Even during a regular check up there is no reliable way to examine the ovaries to see if cancer is on the way.

Although a tremendous amount of research is being done to find the changes that would indicate a danger sign, researchers continue to be puzzled as they look for possible physical changes leading up to the disease.

Before you pull the cover over your head, be aware that you may be receiving certain warning signals.

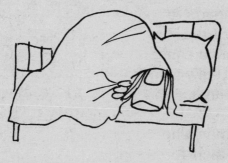

As quiet as the enemy is, even the most silent army is prone to indicate that it has begun to move into position.

Our job is to know what these signs are and to be prepared to take action.

So sound
the bugle
and let's
climb the
ramparts to
see if the
ovarian cancer
cell bully is in
the area.

Women who
are alert for
signs of
danger may
notice symptoms
that suggest all is not right.

These feelings may help a doctor
detect ovarian cancer while it is still
in an early stage.

We are fortunate enough to have a
doctor in the family. My youngest
daughter, Kim, who helped research

this book, was visiting the house
with her husband a few years back.

During the visit,
Kim asked
her mother
how she
was feeling
since she
felt she
looked
tired.

Doreen
mentioned a
periodic slight pain that she had
experienced a few weeks before.

Kim insisted that Doreen push her
regular check-up forward a month.
She did. The result was the
discovery of the early stages of
ovarian cancer. Early enough to be
treated successfully.

Now, not every woman is as lucky. In many cases, by the time symptoms of ovarian cancer have signaled their presence, the disease is already advanced.

One of these signs is abdominal swelling. This swelling is the result of fluid that is beginning to collect in the abdomen.

Months before these symptoms begin to show themselves, however, a woman may begin to complain of problems: indigestion, gassiness, nausea, feeling full after eating a small meal and a loss of appetite.

Many women reading this will immediately say to themselves, "But that's me."

The symptoms I've just described are suffered periodically by most people in today's society and, furthermore, they become more common as we age.

If you want proof of this, just look at the sales figures for medications to help ease gas.

Suffering from indigestion and gas can be annoying. It is, however, not a major problem. Most who suffer a periodic attack ignore the problem, including doctors who hardly take such a complaint seriously.

A popular television commercial sums this up when it shows a

patient explaining her relief after being told to take a well-known, across-the-counter medication to relieve the problem.

If you are over 40 and have a constant problem with any of the above digestive complaints, please do not ignore these irritations.

See your doctor and mention the possibility of ovarian cancer.

Other symptoms can include vaginal bleeding in postmenopausal women or irregular bleeding in women still having periods.

STOP CHECKING
UP ON WHETHER
I'VE HAD A
CHECK UP

Before closing this chapter, let us review the symptoms that may signal the presence of ovarian cancer:

- Abdominal swelling and/or pain.
- Bloating and/or the feeling of fullness.
- Vague but persistent gastrointestinal complaints, such as gas, nausea, indigestion.
- Frequency/urgency of urination.

- Constipation.
- Menstrual disorders, such as abnormal bleeding or postmenopausal bleeding.
- On-going fatigue.
- Pain during intercourse.

These symptoms are most likely indicative of more common benign problems which your doctor will want to exclude first.

This means of eliminating problems will eventually, in most cases, give your doctor the answer as to what the problem may be.

Certainly, the doctor will be anxious to know your medical history. Depending upon the answers you give, he or she will know whether or

not you fall into the category of a
person who is at risk.

What does this mean?

We're about to find out.

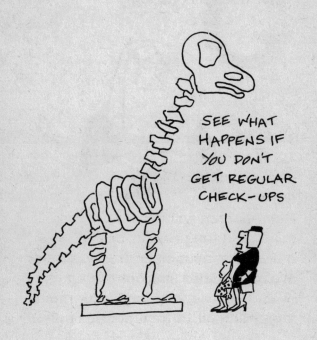

5 WHO IS AT RISK?

In women over the age of 45, about 12 in every 1,000 will develop ovarian cancer.

More women will develop breast, colon and lung cancer but, all too often, ovarian cancer presents itself at a much later stage in the course of the disease, making it that much more difficult to treat successfully.

For this reason, it is absolutely vital that we alert ourselves to the symptoms described in the previous chapter and also to any other risk factors we may have.

As with most diseases, ovarian cancer does follow a pattern that can make a woman believe that her risk of ovarian cancer is more than most women.

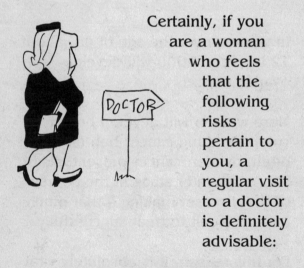

Certainly, if you are a woman who feels that the following risks pertain to you, a regular visit to a doctor is definitely advisable:

• Family history of ovarian cancer, breast cancer or colon cancer.

- Hereditary nonpolyposis colorectal cancer.
- Incessant ovulation (no birth control pill, no pregnancies, infertility).
- Early menopause
- High fat diet (possible)
- Use of high dose estrogen for long periods without progesterone may be a risk factor.

Although these are various factors that may give a woman reason to be particularly conscious of her risk of developing ovarian cancer, the fact is that every woman is at risk regardless of age, heritage or medical history.

AT RISK

Interestingly, family history is where researchers are currently making most of their progress.

Two genes have been identified called the BRCA 1 gene and the BRCA 2 gene which not only increases a woman's risk of developing ovarian cancer but other cancers as well.

There are now a few centres across Canada for women with strong family histories of cancer who can be tested for the presence of the gene.

With this knowledge, women, together with their doctors, can discuss the possible preventive measures they may be able to take.

If your risk of getting the disease is greater than most women, you're going to need to place a close watch on your body.

This is not for you alone. You, and a doctor who understands and appreciates your concerns, must pay close attention. Your doctor is hopefully keen enough in his or her profession to stay up-to-date on your family history and to know whether you are at a high risk of ovarian cancer.

6 FRIEND OR FOE?

So you've got a possible sign or symptom of ovarian cancer.

Before we can take any action, we must be sure that the problem actually exists.

WE'VE FOUND THE PROBLEM

No one wants a leg removed to later find out that the problem was a sprained ankle.

Your doctor will likely order an ultrasound and examine other pelvic organs, looking for a tumour.

The ultrasound is only capable of detecting something that appears different from normal. It has no way of telling us whether it is cancer or not.

For this reason, the next step may be to have a closer look at your ovaries with you on the operating table.

Your doctor may also order some blood work which will likely include a blood test looking for a tumour

marker called CA-125. This tumour
marker is elevated in about 80% of
women with ovarian cancer.

The only true way to know if the
mass discovered is a friend or foe is
through surgery. Since it will be
necessary to look at the cells of the
tumour, a biopsy will be needed.

This can be done by inserting a
long, thin tube with a tiny
telescope, called a laparascope,
through your belly button.

This allows the surgeon to take a look around inside at the problem area.

Although the thoughts of sticking anything inside us can prompt a scream of horror, it is, in many cases, a simple procedure that can be performed on an out-patient basis.

Sometimes, though not always, it's back home the same day with nothing to show but a small bandage over the tiny cut through which the laparascope was inserted.

The surgeon may decide to remove a small piece of tissue for use for biopsy.

If he or she decides that the suspicious growth should be removed entirely to take a closer look, an alternative action may be taken.

A procedure called laparotomy may be decided upon. This will require a much larger abdominal cut.

The next step will be to remove the affected organ or organs -- a hysterectomy, with the removal of both the ovaries and the fallopian tubes.

This procedure can force you to cancel plans for skydiving since it will require a stay of five days in the hospital.

While in hospital, pathologists will examine under microscope the tissues removed during surgery to make a very specific diagnosis.

If everyone is now certain that you have ovarian cancer, it's time to get tough.

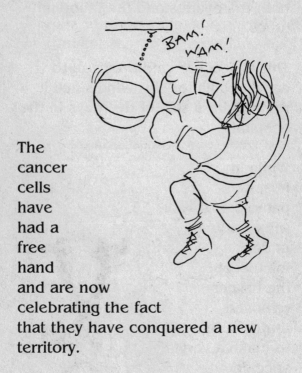

The
cancer
cells
have
had a
free
hand
and are now
celebrating the fact
that they have conquered a new
territory.

After a bang-up party, they'll be set to make plans to take over various other parts of the body.

They're in for a surprise. We're
about to counter-attack and, in fact,
have already taken a major step
toward giving them reasons to regret
picking on your body.

What was this major step?

We went to get professional help.

7 TREATMENT

A whole army of dedicated people is now in our corner, ready to fight. These experts are geared up to take the first step.

As we've said, they will probably begin by removing the diseased ovary or ovaries, as well as the fallopian tubes, the uterus and any visible cancer.

Having tossed them to one side, the surgeon is in a better position to get an overall look at the situation from where they were taken.

Is it clear? Has the disease already begun to move away from its

original camp and gallop into other parts of the country-side?

If so, how far has it reached? To help determine if it has spread, chest x-rays and abdominal CAT scans will be ordered.

Finally, your doctor has all the information he or she needs, and knows that it is ovarian cancer and whether it is still in the ovaries or has spread elsewhere.

The physician takes all this information and is then able to tell you at what stage you are in your disease.

Basically, Stage One signifies that the cancer is only in the ovaries and nowhere else.

Stage Two illustrates that the cancer has been found elsewhere in the body but remains in the pelvis.

Stage Three means that the cancer has spread to the abdomen, whereas Stage Four indicates that the cancer has spread beyond the abdomen or into the liver.

The speed at which the cancer cells work makes it no surprise that diagnosing ovarian cancer at an early stage is difficult.

Classifying all women into a 'stage' makes it easier to plan a course of treatment and also to quickly compare and evaluate what other centres in Canada and around the world are doing to help treat women with similar stages of ovarian cancer.

If you have had your disease confirmed as Stage One, surgery may be sufficient. Some women may be offered radiotherapy.

It is much more likely, however, that you may require chemotherapy, which is medication that is most often delivered through an intravenous into the blood.

This is to help ensure that the medication gets to all the remaining cancer cells and hopefully kills them in their path.

Getting the best treatment is, of course, the answer to any problem. Ovarian cancer is a serious disease and, therefore, needs the best team available.

We know that one of the team players is you. Now all you need is the right partner.

8 GETTING THE RIGHT DOCTOR

Unfortunately, there are few warnings that ovarian cancer has struck, which prompts the question, "If there are no signs that anything is wrong, why see a doctor?"

And if so, which doctor -- the family doctor or a specialist?

Let's start by talking about the family doctor. If you were smart, this doctor would be the one you've been seeing on a regular basis for years.

This doctor would be someone who has given you annual check ups, including internal exams, especially when you became sexually active or pregnant.

So what is a good family doctor? In a nutshell...

One You Can Communicate With

I'm not talking about someone who asks how the family is and then continues to write and use the phone when you're talking.

I'm referring to someone you trust, to whom you can explain your concerns.

This is someone who has become aware of these concerns and has suggested steps to help early detection if there is a problem?

The fact is that not all doctors are like our wonderful Doctor Wu, a family doctor who has served us faithfully for almost 30 years.

To be fair, doctors are human beings. Not all of them feel

comfortable speaking to patients.

The same goes for patients, too. Many of us are uneasy in the presence of doctors and are concerned that we are taking time away from them that could be better spent with someone else.

Just say this to yourself, "I'm the one that's sick." Now ask yourself this, "Do I like this doctor and do I have faith in his or her ability to make me well?"

If the answer is that you feel
unhappy with your doctor, then get
another doctor or a second opinion.

Remember, you're a team.

Fortunately for all of us, most
doctors are caring people who are
genuinely concerned about our
condition.

They know that the medical field
continues to make great strides.

Just know that there are plenty of shoulders to cry on and, if one doctor is concerned about getting his or her shoulder wet, there are plenty who are ready to reach out.

Some women are worried enough to ask themselves whether or not they should visit a specialist.

Finding one who is top in the field of ovarian cancer can be difficult. Even if you do find such a person, he or she may not have the time to see you.

You are someone who is concerned that you may, at a later date, become a victim of the disease.

The specialist that you insist upon seeing is usually in great demand. Putting it bluntly, this specialist is more apt to concentrate efforts on those who are sick.

There is no point in hunting down the top specialist if he or she has little or no time to deal with your concerns.

Which brings us back to the point of choosing the right doctor.

This family doctor and friend will certainly suggest that you have an annual pelvic exam for the rest of your life.

Catching ovarian cancer in the early stages gives us that much better chance of treating the disease with success.

We can do that by teamwork -- you and the doctor you trust.

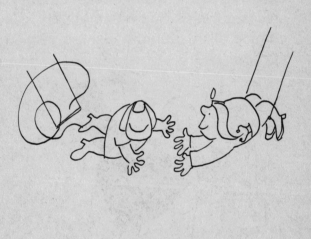

9 YOU STILL HAVE A LIFE TO LEAD

Many have grabbed this book, aware
that they have already received the
lousy news that they have ovarian
cancer.

It is lousy and no amount of
cartoons or flippant remarks are
going to change that fact.

Life goes on, however long or short
it may be.

So what do you want to do with it?

One cancer specialist told me that the answer she gives to a patient who asks, "How long have I got?", is, "How long do you want?"

It may surprise you to know that no one lives for ever.

It is certainly easy to look back on our lives and feel that it is fast coming to an end.

This is not uncommon and feeling this way should not be suppressed.

Try to accept these feelings.

You love
gardening.
So get back
in the garden.
You love
painting.
Drag out the
easel and get
slapping around the oils.

It will not be easy but it will help to
get back to as normal a routine as
you can, even though it may be
difficult to concentrate.

Not all of us are the same or enjoy
doing the same things. It is up to
you to decide on how you can
handle this down period or sadness.

Many of you will have loved ones
who are important in your life.

Continue to enjoy your life with them.

There will be days when you feel that you have been sucked into a blender.

Jump in a tub and have a warm bath.

Take a walk. Sit down to watch the little ones play in a nearby park. Try to enjoy the good things in life.

Have you ever been sky diving? Maybe it's time you did. Want to bungy jump? Try it. You may like it.

Be daring. What the hell have you got to lose? It's time to do, not time to think.

And if you
must think,
think
about
others.

Reach
out.

Upon being told that she had
ovarian cancer, my wife immediately
turned to the surgeon and told him
to get on with whatever it was he
had to do.

"In three months, I have to monitor
the opening of three clinics in Peru,"
she explained to her doctor.

How is Doreen now, four years
later? Great and ready to tackle a
massive job caring for youth in
need of work. The fact is that she
is too busy to worry about herself.

Just look around you.

There really are people who are in need and would welcome what you have to offer.

Use every minute of your time to the fullest.

Does this mean that you'll never again concern yourself with the fact that you have a serious illness?

No, it does not. What it does mean is that these times of concern are less likely to occur than if you were

to sit on a park bench studying
grass growing.

And when these times of worry do
arrive, what then?

We're about to stop helping others
long enough to find out.

10 WHAT HAPPENS NEXT?

Although your treatment is behind you, there comes a time for all those who have cancer to be concerned.

The surgeon said, "We got it all". But did he? And if he or she did 'get it all', how come you suddenly feel a little pain in your side?

Within seconds you find yourself on the phone to your doctor, "Is this right what I feel?"

"Does this mean the treatment has not worked?"

First, we should know that we are no different to any other patient who has been through the experience of treatment for cancer.

Let's face it. You have not been in bed with a lousy cold or fever.

So how do we overcome these anxious moments? Shifting your mind toward others in need will shove concerns for ourself back into the recesses of our mind.

Although it may be hard to understand, many people who have experienced cancer found it to be a turning point in their lives.

They were suddenly faced with their own mortality -- in a way they had never known before.

They changed direction and found a fuller and more content way of spending their time on earth.

In the meantime, enjoy life to the fullest and use it wisely.

Corinne Boyer Fund was established in 1996 to address the neglect surrounding the "disease that whispers" and embraces a two-fold mission: raising awareness about cancer of the ovary and increasing financial and educational resources for medical and personal efforts to prevent and successfully treat ovarian cancer.

Corinne Boyer Fund is rapidly claiming a strong leadership position in Canada against cancer of the ovary, through bold initiatives including establishment, in January 1998, of the first Chair in ovarian cancer research at the University of Ottawa. The Corinne Boyer Research Laboratory will also be dedicated to ovarian cancer. Other programs include support groups for women with ovarian cancer, Lunch and Learn sessions, and an Ovarian Cancer Resource Network.

For more information on any of these programs, please contact
Corinne Boyer Fund at:
620 University Avenue, Toronto, CA M5G 2L7

Tel: (416) 971-9800 · Fax: (416) 971-6888
Email: cbf@cancercare.on.ca

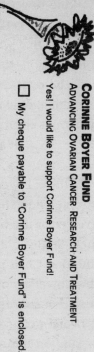

CORINNE BOYER FUND
ADVANCING OVARIAN CANCER RESEARCH AND TREATMENT

Yes! I would like to support Corinne Boyer Fund!

☐ My cheque payable to "Corinne Boyer Fund" is enclosed.

Please bill my ☐ VISA ☐ MASTERCARD Card Number: _____

Amount: $ _____ Expiry Date: _____ Signature: _____

I would like to order _____ copies of this book @ $4.00 per copy (includes postage and handling).

Name _____

Address _____

City _____ Province _____ Postal Code _____

620 University Avenue, Toronto, Canada M5G 2L7 • (416) 971-9800 • Fax (416) 971-6888 • cbf@cancercare.on.ca

A charitable tax receipt will be issued for donations.